My
Favorite
Horses

WILD
HORSES

Stephanie Turnbull

A⁺
Smart Apple Media

Published by Smart Apple Media,
an imprint of Black Rabbit Books
P.O. Box 3263, Mankato, Minnesota, 56002
www.blackrabbitbooks.com

Designed by Hel James
Edited by Mary-Jane Wilkins

Cataloging-in-Publication Data is available from the Library of Congress

ISBN 978-1-62588-185-4

Photo acknowledgements
l = left, r = right, t = top, b = bottom
title page justasc/Shutterstock; page 3 Makarova Viktoria/Shutterstock;
4-5 alersandr hunta/Shutterstock; 6-7 Olga_i/Shutterstock; 8-9, 10,
11 all iStockphoto/Thinkstock; 12-13 Bernhard Richter/Shutterstock;
14-15 Jeanne Provost/Shutterstock; 16 Daniel Gale; 17 Gerard
Koudenburg/both Shutterstock; 18 Johann Helgason; 19 Scott
E Read/both Shutterstock; 20-21 Gertjan Hooijer; 21b J. Marijs/
both Shutterstock; 22 Pierre-Jean Durieu; 23 Lilac Mountain/
both Shutterstock
Cover iStock/Thinkstock

Printed in China

DAD0055
032014
9 8 7 6 5 4 3 2 1

Contents

Running Free

Some horses never wear saddles, carry riders, or sleep in stables.

They live wild in remote places all over the world.

Many wild horses roam across grassy plains. They must find their own food, water, and shelter.

Going Wild

In the past, some horses were lost or abandoned by their owners, and learned to survive on their own.

Most wild horses today are related to these horses.

Another name for them is feral horses.

They are strong, sturdy… and a little untidy!

Real Wild Horses

Przewalski horses (say "sheh-val-skee") are the only *real* wild horses in the world.

No one has ever owned or tamed these horses.

Przewalski horses come from
Mongolia. Small groups live
in the wild and in zoos.

Mighty Mustangs

Mustangs are wild horses that live in the dusty deserts of western North America.

Every day they walk for miles across the rocky land, searching for patches of grass to eat and water to drink.

Outback Brumbies

Australia has more wild horses than anywhere else in the world. They are called Brumbies.

Some Australians think Brumbies are pests as they trample plants and damage trees. Others think they are an important part of the country's history.

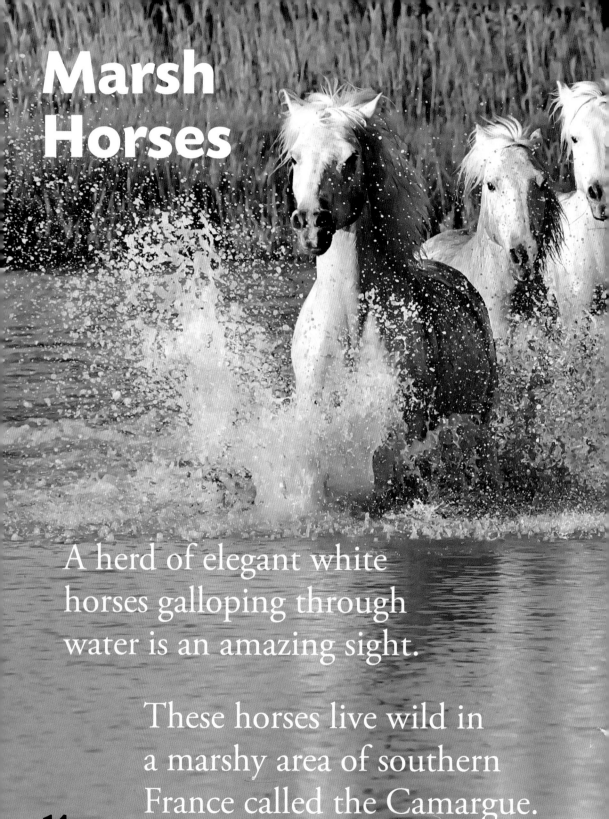

Marsh Horses

A herd of elegant white horses galloping through water is an amazing sight.

These horses live wild in a marshy area of southern France called the Camargue.

They have extra-wide hooves
to help them walk on the soft,
squishy ground. Sometimes
they swim instead!

Wild Families

Wild horses live in small family groups of one stallion, a few mares, and their young. Foals stay close to their mother until they are two or three years old.

Horses nudge, nuzzle, or gently nip each other.

Fierce Fighters

Sometimes stallions fight to see who is the strongest. They strike out with their front legs.

Stallions will also kick and bite other animals who want to harm their family. This cougar could kill a young Mustang.

A Tough Life

Living outdoors isn't easy!
Winters can be bitterly cold, with
swirling blizzards and heavy snow.

Summers can be hot
and sticky, with clouds
of biting insects.

Wild horses
eat anything
they can find
in winter,
even tree bark.

Taming and Training

Farmers sometimes train wild horses to pull carts or carry riders. They make good workers because they are tough and sure-footed.

Farmers use Camargue horses to herd cattle.

Some people rescue hurt
or starving Mustangs and
turn them into riding horses.

Useful Words

feral Living in a wild, untamed way.

mare An adult female horse.

plain A big area of open, flat land with few trees.

stallion An adult male horse.

Index